With a rich mix of cool c
reign as a proud centre
cultural life. Here, the lei
contrast the city's effici
able and accessible throu........ ....., ... it hard to imagine
a more livable place than this Austrian capital.

CITIx60: Vienna explores the cultural heart of Austria in five aspects,
covering architecture, art spaces, shops and markets, eating and
entertainment. With expert advice from 60 stars of the city's creative scene, this book guides you to the genuine attractions of the
city for a taste of blissful Vienna life.

Contents

Before You Go

BASIC INFO

Currency
Euro (EUR/€)
Exchange rate: €1 : $1.2

Time zone
GMT +1
DST +2

DST begins at 0200 (local time) on the last Sunday of March and ends at 0300 (local time) on the last Sunday of October.

Dialling
International calling: +43
Citywide (0)1*

*Dial (0) for calls made within Austria.

Weather (avg. temperature range)
Spring (Feb-May): 6-15°C / 43-59°F
Summer (June-Aug): 18-20°C / 64-68°F
Autumn (Sept-Nov): 5-16°C / 41-61°F
Winter (Dec-Feb): -2-3°C / 28-37°F

USEFUL WEBSITE

U-Bahn, tramway network & most Bus routes
www.wienerlinien.at

EMERGENCY CALLS

Ambulance
144

Fire
122

Police
133

Embassies
China   +43 (0)1 710 3648
France   +43 (0)1 502 752 14
Germany   +43 (0)1 711 540
Japan   +43 (0)1 531 920
UK   +43 (0)1 716 130
US   +43 (0)1 313 390

AIRPORT EXPRESS TRANSFER

**Flughafen Wien <-> Wien Mitte
(City Airport Train)**
Train / Journey: every 30 mins / 16 mins
From Flughafen Wien: 0606-2336 daily
From Wien Mitte: 0536-2306 daily
One-way: €12 / Return: €19
www.cityairporttrain.com

Flughafen Wien <-> Wien Morzinplatz (Bus 1185)
Bus / Journey: every 30 mins / 20-22 mins
From Flughafen Wien: 0450-0020, 0120, 0250 daily
From Wien Morzinplatz: 0400-2330, 0030, 0200 daily
One-way: €8/4
www.postbus.at/en/Airportbus/Vienna_Airport-Lines/Morzinplatz/index.jsp

PUBLIC TRANSPORT IN VIENNA

Subway (U-bahn)
Train (S-Bahn)
Tram (Straßenbahn)
Bus (Autobus)

Means of Payment
Credit cards (ticketing)
Cash

GENERAL PUBLIC HOLIDAYS

January	1 New Year's Day, 6 Epiphany
March/April	Easter Monday
May/June	1 Labour Day, Ascension Day, Whit Monday, Corpus Christi
August	15 Assumption Day
October	26 National Day
November	1 All Saints' Day
December	8 Immaculate Conception, 25 Christmas Day, 26 St. Stephen's Day

Museums and galleries here normally open on public holidays but special hours apply. Shops and restaurants likely take summer breaks between June and August.

FESTIVALS / EVENTS

May
MuseumsQuartier Summer (through to September)
www.mqw.at

June
Vienna Pride
www.viennapride.at
Vienna Biennale (through to October)
www.viennabiennale.org
Wiener Staatsoper Live Outdoors (through to September)
www.wiener-staatsoper.at

July
dotdotdot film festival (though to August)
www.dotdotdot.at
Freihausviertel Festival
freihausviertel.at

August
ImPulsTanz Dance Festival
www.impulstanz.com

September
Vienna Design Week (through to October)
www.viennadesignweek.at
Open House Vienna
openhouse-wien.at
Waves Vienna Festival (through to October)
www.wavescentraleurope.com
MQ Vienna Fashion Week
www.viennafashionweek.com

October
Long Night of the Museums
langenacht.orf.at
Vienna Internatioanl Film Festival (through to November)
www.viennale.at
Waves Vienna
www.wavescentraleurope.com

November
Vienna Art Week
FB: Vienna Art Week

Event days vary by year. Please check for updates online.

UNUSUAL OUTINGS

MAK ON TOUR
mak.at/en/program/events/mak_on_tour

Bike Experience Vienna
www.trekkingaustria.com

PolaWalk
www.polawalk.com/en

Trekking Austria
www.trekkingaustria.com

SMARTPHONE APP

Austrian cuisine explained
Master Order

Bike route & real-time navigator
Bike Citizens

Integrated route-planner
qando Vienna

U-Bahn map & route planner
Vienna Transport Map

REGULAR EXPENSES

A cup of coffee at Kaffeehäuser
€3-5

Domestic / International mail (postcards)
€0.68/1.7

Gratuities
At restaurants, bars & cafés: Round up to the nearest Euro
At hotels: €1 @bag for the porter and €1@night for housekeeper
On licensed taxis: 5-10% of payment

Count to 10

What makes Vienna so special?

Illustrations by Guillaume Kashima aka Funny Fun

Comfortably paced, but never outdated, it is the easy-going Viennese spirit that dominates the city. Repeatedly ranked as one of the world's most livable city, Vienna is a place where you can enjoy green spaces, coffee and cakes and recharge through the sophisticated visual beauty. Whether you are on a one-day stopover or a week-long stay, see what Vienna creatives consider essential to see, taste, read and take home from your trip.

1

Architecture

Wirtschaftspark Breitensee
by HOLODECK Architects

Karl Marx-Hof
by Karl Ehn

Haus Wittgenstein (#11)
by Paul Engelmann & Ludwig Wittgenstein

Gewerbehof Mollardgasse
by Otto Richter & Leopold Ramsauer

Flaktürme
by Friedrich Tamms

Kugelmugel
By Edwin Lipburger

# 2	# 3	# 4
Museums & Galleries	**Parks & Gardens**	**Traditional Coffee Houses**

Museums & Galleries

Urban art
Inoperable Gallery
www.inoperable.at

Modern & contemporary art
TBA21 (#15)
Secession, www.secession.at
MUMOK, www.mumok.at

Art brut (Outsider art)
Museum Gugging
www.gugging.at

Hunderwasser's work
Kunst Haus &
Hundertwasserhaus
www.kunsthauswien.com

Architecture & urban design
Architekturzentrum Wien
www.azw.at

Gallery district
Schleifmühlgasse

Parks & Gardens

Burggarten
Palmenhaus (#47) & the Butterfly House
www.schmetterlinghaus.at

Sankt Marxer Friedhof
Mozart's grave & smell of lilac in spring
www.wien.gv.at

Prater
Centuries old ferris wheel &
117m swing carousel
prater.at

Schönbrunn
Imperial summer residence &
"the world's oldest zoo"
www.zoovienna.at

Lainzer Tiergarten
Primitive wood, wild boar & deers
www.lainzer-tiergarten.at

Steinhofgründe
Walking trails, ponds & meadows

Traditional Coffee Houses

Café Prückel (est. 1903)
Oswald Haerdtl architecture &
appetitbrot
www.prueckel.at

Café Sperl (est. 1880)
Before Sunrise (1995) film scene
www.cafesperl.at

Café Bräunerhof
Thomas Bernhard's favourite
haunt
Stallburggasse 2, 1010

Café Schwarzenberg (est. 1861)
Live music & traditional offerings
www.cafe-schwarzenberg.at

Café Museum (est. 1899)
Adolf Loos interior
www.cafemuseum.at

Café Landtmann (est. 1873)
Sigmund Freud's favourite spot
www.landtmann.at

5

Heurigen

Göbel
www.weinbaugoebel.at

Mayer am Pfarrplatz
www.pfarrplatz.com

Zahel
www.zahel.at

Weinhof Zimmermann
www.weinhof-zimmermann.at

Weingut am Reisenberg
www.weingutamreisenberg.at

Zum Berger
www.zumberger.at

Sirbu
sirbu.at

Schübel-Auer
www.schuebel-auer.at

6

Savouries

Leberkäsesemmel (meat loaf buns)
Fleischerei Ringl
Gumpendorfer Str., 105
(Horse meat edition) Rudolf Schuller
Reinprechtsdorfer Str. 9, 1050

Schnitzel (fried cutlets)
(Veal cutlets) Gasthaus Pöschl
Weihburggasse 17, 1010
(Pork cutlets) Figlmüller
www.figlmueller.at

Dry cured Mangalitsa bacon
Lokal Nuss
Schopenhauer Str. 19 (corner Kutschkergasse), 1180

Coriander Bosna
Bitzinger
www.bitzinger-wien.at

Käsekrainer (Cheese-filled sausage)
Alles Walzer, Alles Wurst
Quellenstr. 84, 1100

7

Desserts & Confectioneries

Apfelstrudel (Apple strudels)
Café Korb (#38)

Buchteln (Sweet yeast buns)
Café Hawelka
www.hawelka.at

Eis-marillenknödel (Ice apricot balls)
Tichy, www.tichy-eis.at

Zaunerkipferl (Sweet nut croissants)
Bakery GRIMM, www.grimm.at

Nougat ice-cream
Eissalon, www.gelato.at

Esterházy-Schnitte (layered cakes) / Topfengolatsche (curd cheese pockets)
AIDA Cafés, aida.at

Petits-fours
Fruth, www.fruth.at

8

Music

Mozart's apartment
Mozarthaus
www.mozarthausvienna.at

Haydn's residence
Haydnhaus
www.wienmuseum.at/en/
locations/haydnhaus.html

Viennese piano
Bösendorfer
www.boesendorfer.com

Thrift record store
Teuchtler Schallplattenhandel &
Antiquariat
teuchtler.businesscard.at

Music & ballet performances
Wiener Staatsoper
www.wiener-staatsoper.at

**Make an analogue vinyl with
Flabbergasting Record Elevator**
SuperSense Palace
the.supersense.com

9

Cinemas

Theatre, bar & café
Schikaneder
www.schikaneder.at

Historic cinema
Gartenbaukino (#56)

Film-related museum
The Third Man
www.3mpc.net/engl_orson_
welles.htm

Cinema of old German films
Bellaria
www.film.at/bellaria_kino

Austrian Film Museum
Österreichisches Filmmuseum
www.filmmuseum.at

Austrian Film Archive
Metro Kinokulturhaus
www.metrokino.at

10

Day Trip
*recommended by
Wolfgang Lehrner*

Swim at the 1920s Amalienbad
Reumannpl. 23, 1100

Explore another Vienna
Favoritenstr. (car-free zone)

**Drop by Wien Hauptbahnhof,
take a look from Platform 3 &
leave at the east entrance**
Am Hauptbahnhof 1, 1100

Go see 21er Haus (#13)
Visit Belvedere Schlossgarten
& exit at the Lower Belvedere
www.belvedere.at

**Enter Innere Stadt & get lost
within the tiny streets**
1st district

Stroll along Donaukanal (#12)

Get to Leopoldstadt
*Former Jewish district & the
hippest part of the city*

Icon Index

 Opening hours

 Address

 Contact

 Remarks

 Admission

Facebook

URL Website

 Scan QR codes to access Google Maps and discover the area around each destination. Internet connection required.

60x60

60 Local Creatives x 60 Hotspots

From vast cityscapes to the tiniest glimpses of everyday life, Vienna offers unrelenting provocation of one's imagination. 60x60 points you to 60 haunts where 60 arbiters of taste go for the good stuff.

Landmarks & Architecture   SPOTS · 01 – 12 📍

Viennese architecture is well mixed with art and the city's imperial history. Take in the city with a relaxed pace. A bottle of wine or a picnic basket always makes for great company.

Cultural & Art Spaces   SPOTS · 13 – 24 📍

Prepare to experience arts with new eyes and new ears. Be sure to add original plays and street art to your contemporary art walk for a full experience.

Markets & Shops   SPOTS · 25 – 36 📍

Neubau is for shoppers of all types, whether you're into photography or fashion. Look out for the tailor-made as much as the readymade. Some treasures can only be found in town.

Restaurants & Cafés   SPOTS · 37 – 48 📍

Vienna's culinary culture celebrates the traditional and welcomes the new. Visit age-old coffee houses, wine taverns and select hotspots serving excellent international cuisine.

Nightlife   SPOTS · 49 – 60 📍

Classic movies, hip parties and refreshing drinks take over Vienna's nights. Formal attire might not be called for a great evening outing but no music ever spins off the cuff.

Landmarks & Architecture

Top notch learning facilities, brave Viennese builds and the Danube

From religious and residential establishments to retail spaces, parks and cafés, Vienna's architecture is outstanding witness to a constant interchange of values that are hard to separate from other spheres of art. Philosophers, designers, sculptors and visual artists contentedly applied their own artistic visions into the built environment, engendering a unique cityscape next to important examples of Baroque, Romanesque, Classicist, Art Nouveau and Wiener Moderne in and around the city's recognised historic centre, a UNESCO world heritage site since 2001.

The architectural riches of Vienna can be appreciated in many leisurely ways. One of which is by jumping on the Ring Tram Circuit to view the iconic St. Stephen's cathedral, the Secession and Otto Wagner's Postal Savings Bank (#10) next to less obvious gems like Hans Hollein's candle shop (#6) bound by the line of the demolished city walls from the 19th century. Wine lovers should follow the Viennese and enjoy a slow Sunday afternoon with a glass of wine and with the remarkable cityscape at one of the heurigen on Kahlenberg (#7) or at the top of DC Tower 1 (#1). Look out for Open House Vienna (*openhouse-wien.at*) if you come in the autumn. Fervent architecture fans, be sure you include Architekturzentrum Wien (*www.azw. at*) on your itinerary.

Florian "Doc" Kaps
Co-founder, Supersense

I am deeply in love with everything analogue. After "The Impossible Project", an attempt to save the last Polaroid factory, Supersense celebrates touch in Dogenhof on Praterstrasse.

DC Towers
P.014

Wirtschafts-
universität
Wien
P.016

Erwin K. Bauer
Founder, buero bauer

I'm the creative mind at buero bauer, a interdisciplinary design studios. I teach at the Academy of Applied Arts Vienna, also curate Typopassage and the Labor at Vienna Design Week.

Chris Precht
Founding partner, penda

I'm the head of penda with offices in Vienna and Beijing. We reinterpret historical architecture of both cities in a responsible, ecological and fresh light. I've been living in Vienna since 2010.

Schloss
Wilhelminen-
berg
P.018

Matthias Lautner
Artist

I am a painter born in Vienna in 1981. I enjoy taking a stroll around the city before returning to the solitude of my studio. My latest shows took place at Kubin-Haus and Bäckerstraße 4 Gallery.

Rudolf-
Bednar-Park
P.019

Trabrennbahn
Krieau
P.020

meshit
Fashion label

We are Lena and Ida, both bred and living in Vienna. We've been running meshit together since 2010, after graduating from the fashion school of Vienna, Hetzendorf.

Mohammad Ali Ziaei
Caricaturist

I was born and brought up in Tehran, Iran. Since 2002, I reside in Vienna where I attended the University of Applied Art and studied industrial design.

Retti
P.021

Martina B. Cerny
Founder, Making Of

I was born in Munich, but the uniqueness of Vienna made me stay. I've been here for over 30 years, and I own a make-up, hair and styling agency called Making Of.

Augarten
P.023

Snoww Crystal
Band

Snoww Crystal is from Vienna. Our music blends dreamy walls of guitars, repetitive rhythms, sweet vocal melodies and hypnotic synth patterns. Ethereal, eerie and wintry.

Eva Buchleitner
Designer, EVA BLUT

I am the designer of EVA BLUT. We make bags and accessories in a post-minimalist style that are extremely light and functional but look iconic.

Kahlenberg
P.022

Wotruba-
kirche
P.024

Daniel Gebhart de Koekkoek, *Photographer*

I started my career in 2006, interned at Magnum Photos, and have worked for the likes of Vanity Fair and Monocle. My first book was awarded "PDN Best Photo Books of the Year" in 2014.

Haus
Wittgenstein
P.026

Thomas Geisler
Design curator, MAK

A constant critical mind actively following the local and international design scenes, especially since I co-founded Vienna Design Week. I am a non-native now calling Vienna home.

Inoperable Gallery
Art gallery

Nicholas Platzer and Nathalie Halgand form Inoperable, specialising in presenting contemporary art emerging from urban subcultures since 2006.

Österr.
Postsparkasse
P.025

Donaukanal
P.027

1 DC Towers
Map K, P.109

At a height of 250 meters tall, DC Tower 1 is a monolith within Vienna's topology. Designed by French architect Dominique Perrault and realised as the first and taller of two, the edifice stands perpendicular to the historic city with an undulating front reflecting on river Danube and the metallic umbrellas to soften the wind on the ground. Sixty storeys are inhabited by a hotel, offices, lofts and dining facilities, bordered by the UN offices, Hollein's Saturn Tower and science and technology park, Tech Gate. The cluster constitutes the new sustainable, multifunctional district, Donau City.

Donau-City-Str., 1220
URL www.viennadc.at

"Check out the towers from 3 different eras: Hochhaus, Vienna's first 'skyscraper' at Herrengasse 6–8, Toboggan in Prater and experience height at DC Tower 1's skybar!"

– Florian "Doc" Kaps, Supersense

2 Wirtschaftsuniversität Wien
Map J, P.108

High profile international architects Zaha Hadid, Atelier Hitoshi Abe, NO.MAD and CRABstudio vivify the Vienna University of Economics and Business as they added six imposing and innovative buildings onto its new 9-hectare site in Leopoldstadt. Local firm BUSarchitektur has envisioned the learning space as a "walk along park", offering substantial green open space, restaurants and shops for students and teachers to interact. Access the campus through one of the three different entrances near the Vienna Fair (Messe Wien) plaza, on Trabrennstraße or from the Prater Park side. Cafeteria Mensa in D1 is another futuristically designed highlight.

🏠 Welthandelspl. 1, 1020
📞 +43 (0)1 313 360 🔗 www.wu.ac.at

"Just next to the Campus on Trabrennstraße, you can find the Stadtbiotop (www.stadtbiotop.at), a container pop-up village that houses interesting small shops."

– Erwin K. Bauer, buero bauer

3 Schloss Wilhelminenberg
Map T, P.111

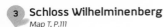

Named after one of the aristocratic owners, but formerly called "Gallitzinerberg", this 120,000 square metre park surrounding Castle Wilhelminenberg wasn't always a beautiful sight. This historic scene has had its share of dark and controversial moments when it was a military hospital during the war periods and an orphanage for girls in the 1920s. Nowadays it has been transformed to a four-star hotel under the brand of "Austria Trend Hotels". Most of the area is still publicly accessible so visitors can enjoy the green space for a picnic or a walk. The neighbouring Schottenwald has great hiking trails.

🏠 *Savoyenstr. 2, 1160* 🕐 *+43 (0)1 485 8503*
🔗 *www.austria-trend.at/Hotel-Schloss-Wilhelminenberg/en*

"In case you are a hiking fan, the neighbouring Schottenwald offers inviting trails for a jaunt around its rolling landscape."

– Chris Precht, penda

4 Rudolf-Bednar-Park

Map Q, P.110

Where most of Vienna displays a labyrinthine complexity of organic towns, the landscaped park may be a welcome difference in the city's new urban area, Danube. Named after Leopoldstadt's ex-district chairman, Rudolf-Bednar-Park is a competition winning design by Swiss landscape architect Guido Hager, who conceived a curtained-off community space that offers opportunity to cycle, skate and simply hanging out over the expansive lawns and waterbounded paths. The project was part of an improvement programme subsidised by the EU and realised over the former site of Vienna's North Station.

🏠 Vorgartenstr., 1020

> "*Come here for the interesting contrast with Vienna's major developments. Combine your visit with a walk through Augarten and TBA21 (#15).*"
>
> – Matthias Lautner

5 Trabrennbahn Krieau
Map J, P.108

Visiting the Krieau and the racetrack is always nostalgic for the Viennese. While the golden days of skully racing, horse jockeys and high-society members with grand hats is certainly over, you can still watch peculiar locals trying their luck with their bets at the century-old Krieau, home of the Viennese Harness Racing Club. Whilst there, enjoy Europe's first steel and concrete grandstand built by architect Otto Wagner's students in 1913. Racing season runs from September to June. When the horses are on their summer break, the Krieau segues into a concert venue or open-air cinema showing classical movies.

🏠 Nordportalstr. 247, 1020
URL www.krieau.at

"Go on a Sunday and place a bet. Here you can meet extraordinary Viennese people."
– meshit

6 Retti
Map B, P.104

Comissioned by candle retailer Retti in 1966, this silvery boutique shop notably encapsulates architect and designer Hans Hollein's (1934–2014) postmodernism aesthetics. From the sci-fi looking entrance to the bespoke lighting and the elegant display cases, geometric forms jostle with a curtain of anodised aluminium to absorb shoppers on one of Vienna's busiest shopping streets. The shop's current occupient is jeweller Gadner. Steps away find Schullin's glittering outlet at Kohlmarkt 18, another trademark design by Hollein completed in 1974.

🕙 *Gadner: 1000–1300, 1400–1800 (M–F), –1700 (Sa)*
🏠 *Kohlmarkt 10, 1010* **URL** *www.hollein.com*

"*Candle shop Retti is simply one of the most amazing buildings in Vienna built in the 1960s.*"

– Mohammad Ali Ziaei

7 Kahlenberg
Map R, P.111

Just a 30 minute drive or short bus ride from the city centre, you'll already feel like you're in rural Austria. From the 484 metres tall "house hill", enjoy a spectacular view over the city's vineyards and skyline. On a clear day you will see the Schneeberg in the distance, source of the famously pure Vienna drinking water. Kahlenberg is home to many "heurigen", where local winemakers serve seasonal wine and regional dishes. Immerse into the area's gemütlichkeit, order wine and unwind in these foothills of the Alps.

🏠 *Am Kahlenberg, 1190*
URL *www.kahlenberg-wien.at*

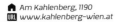

"Visit Kahlenberg by both day and night for the equally stunning views. You should definitely enjoy a glass of wine in one of Vienna's famous 'heurigen'."

– Martina B. Cerny, Making Of

8 Augarten
Map I, P.108

Originally built as a hunting lodge, the Augarten is a witness to Vienna's changes and has been the city's cultural hub since the early 17th century. Fifty some hectares of space hosts the city's oldest French Baroque park, Europe's second oldest porcelain manufactory, the Austrian Film Archive, and the rehearsal venue of the renown Vienna Boys' Choir. Mozart, Beethoven, Schubert, and Strauss all acted as conductors or composers here at one point. Standing starkly at two ends of the park are two of the six monstrous anti-aircraft bunkers (*Flaktürme*), relics of WWII. The one in Ester-házypark has been home to a public aquarium since 1957.

🕐 *0630 till dusk daily (Apr–Oct), 0730– (Nov–Mar)*
🏠 *Gaußpl. 11, 1020* 📞 *+43 (0)1 877 5087*
🔗 *www.bmlfuw.gv.at (DE)*

"In summer every year, there's also an open air cinema. Go there on a sunny summer day and relax on the meadows."

– Snoww Crystal

9 **Wotrubakirche**
Map S, P.111

Designed by sculptor Fritz Wotruba (1907–75) and realised with architect Fritz Gerhard Mayr's technical support, this walk-in sculpture is ample reason to visit Liesing on the southwest edge of Vienna. Planned as a church without a specific site in mind, the 152 seemingly random stack of raw cement chunks manifest the artist's belief in finding beauty in simplicity. Feel Wotruba's ambition as you enter the structure. On the altar wall is a replica of the Wotruba cross created for Hofkirche in Bruchsal, Germany.

🕓 1400–2000 (Sa), 0900–1630 (Su & P.H.)
🏠 Ottillingerpl. 1, 1230   ☎ +43 (0)1 888 6147
🔲 www.georgenberg.at

"This church stands as a building as well as a sculpture. The surrounding area is nice to walk around if you need a break from the city."

– Eva Buchleitner, EVA BLUT

10 Österr. Postsparkasse
Map O, P.110

Completed in 1912 by Viennese architect Otto Wagner (1841–1918), the Austrian Postal Savings Bank is a historic icon in many ways. Utilitarian function of a strongbox was graphically enhanced by clean forms and modern materials, marking the architect's daring departure from Art Nouveau and Neoclassicism to modernism. Architectural highlights include the marble-clad façade affixed with aluminium-covered metal bolts, the light-filled hall constructed of frosted glass and polished steel and its furniture. It still houses the headquarters of the bank but is supplemented by a museum entirely dedicated to Wagner's life and work.

🏠 Georg-Coch-Pl. 2, 1018
🔗 Wagner: Werk Museum Postsparkasse: 1000–1700 (M–F), €6/4, www.ottowagner.com

"It's simply great architecture."
– Daniel Gebhart de Koekkoek

11 Haus Wittgenstein
Map H, P.107

Also known as Stonborough House, the Wittgenstein Haus is architect Paul Engelmann's (1891–1965) only built project, realised in hands with philosopher Ludwig Wittgenstein (1889–1951) as commissioned by his sister. Modernist traits are as evident as they were when it was completed in 1928, reflecting Wittgenstein's persistence in acquiring perfect proportions across the house's finishing touches and Adolf Loos' influences on Engelmann. The house made a narrow escape from being demolished and was declared a national monument in 1971.

🕑 *1000–1200, 1500–1630 (M-F & by appointment)*
🏠 *Parkgasse 18, 1030* 📞 *+43 (0)1 713 3164*
URL *www.haus-wittgenstein.at*

"Since it houses the Bulgarian Cultural Institute today, it is publicly accessible. But it is off the beaten track. Watch out for the opening hours."

– Thomas Geisler, MAK

12 Donaukanal
Map E, P.106

Walk down to the waterside promenade at Schwedenplatz, and go to wherever looks most interesting along the Danube Canal. Since Vienna discovered the Danube, which flows from Germany, the city and leisure activities thrive along the 17-kilometre waterway for Viennese to enjoy the warm summer nights. walk along the banks of the canal and tuck into one of the many ever changing bars on offer. There's something for every taste, whether you want a beach party vibe at Tel Aviv or a piece of the Mediterranean at Pub Klemo as Wasser. If you have a bit more time, you can even take a boat to Bratislava, Vienna's close Slovakian neighbour.

🏠 Schwedenplatz, 1010
🔗 To Bratislava: www.twincityliner.com, €20–35

"It's a great place to see a ton of graffiti/street art! Explore the numerous options to take boat trips along the Donaukanal leaving from Schwedenplatz."

– Nathalie Halgand & Nicholas Platzer, Inoperable Gallery

Cultural & Art Spaces

Specialist art institutions, unequalled programmes and creations

The arts are Vienna's biggest asset. From the palatial grand buildings lining the Ringstrasse, combined with modern hotspots of urban subculture and the artistic treasures dating back centuries, the city's rich history can be experienced through a truly vast and diverse cultural offering. It is easy to stumble upon the grand permanent collection of oil paintings and drawings as well as contemporary exhibitions at Albertina (#22). Nearby you'll find the Spanish Riding School (www.srs.at) an impressive 450-year old institution adorned in Baroque era architecture and home to a cavalry of Lipizzaner horses. Just a short walk south of Ringstrasse, explore Vienna's MuseumsQuartier, one of the world's largest cultural art complexes, housing over 70 different facilities. The Secession (www.secession.at) on Friedrichstraße features the movement's artwork by the likes of Gustav Klimt.

Be sure to balance traditional cultural experiences in the city with the more casual ones. Formerly the Anker bread bakery (#19) is a patchwork of art, photography, vintage and events. Or combine an art show with architectural sight seeing in a stroll through the clean 50s architecture gallery of the 21er Haus (#13). Or drop into Rabbit Eye Movement Gallery (#18) and you will get street art, illustration and a beer.

For the evening you might want to opt for one of the theatre houses, such as Schauspielhaus (#21) where you can view innovative plays. Alternatively, immerse yourself in magnificence of the Opera House, being serenaded by Vienna's famous philharmonic.

Madame Mohr
Creative collective

Comprised of architects, designers and machines, Madame Mohr investigates ethics and aesthetics on all scales. We offer design and consulting services in rendering and animation.

Wiener Art Foundation
P.033

Klemens Torggler
Visual artist

Brought up in Innsbruck I moved to Vienna in 1983 to study art. Painting is the main focus of my artistic work. I create kinetic art objects based on a flip panel door system I invented in 1997.

mischer'traxler studio
Industrial design duo

Katharina Mischer and Thomas Traxler design objects and more with focuses on experiments, conceptual thinking and the balance between handcraft and technology.

21er Haus
P.032

TBA21
P.034

Klaus Mühlbauer
Hatter & milliner, Mühlbauer

I'm the fourth generation to run the family-owned hat business, and I've been doing so since 2001. During the last few years we've taken out hats out of Vienna, selling them all over the world.

MAK
P.038

Fabienne Feltus
Art director, Bureau F

I manage Bureau F with Philipp Stürzenbecher. We build brands in the fields of culture, cuisine, lifestyle, fashion and art. Unmistakable aesthetics and function are our trademarks.

WILD
Interactive design agency

WILD specialises in conception, design and the development of innovative campaigns, websites and apps. We love playing tabletop soccer and beer. If you're thirsty, just join us in our office.

Kunst-historisches Museum
P.036

Rabbit Eye Movement
P.040

DMAA
Architectural firm

Founded in 1993, Delugan Meissl Associated Architects have many remarkable social housing and cultural building projects under their belt, among them the Beam (AT) and EYE Film (NL).

Arena
P.042

GIANTREE
Band

GIANTREE have always had a knack for combining grand emotions with a grand sound. Their EP "Densest Black" fuels expectations regarding the difficult second record.

Hubert Weinheimer
Musician & writer

I am originally from rural Austria and have lived in Vienna since 2003. I released two albums as the bandleader of "Das trojanische Pferd" and, in 2014, published the novel "Gui Gui".

Ankerbrot-fabrik
P.041

Schauspiel-haus
P.044

Creative-Mornings Vienna
P.046

Katie Gruber
Jewellery designer, Katie g.

I'm British born and raised in Vienna. After finding my passion and studying jewellery design in Florence, I started my own label in Vienna. I create and sell from my atelier in the 7th district.

Alice Katter
Social media strategist, moodley

After living in London for two years, the Austrian charm brought me back to Vienna, a city full of opportunities, creative spirit and energy.

Andreas Scheiger
Art director

I'm an art director by profession and an explorer of art and culture by passion. I always like handicraft, drawing and experimenting. It's about the joy of bringing things into existence.

Albertina
P.045

Stadtschrift
P.047

13 21er Haus
Map M, P.109

Initially designed by Karl Schwanzer (1918–75) to showcase Austria at EXPO Brussels 1958, this modernist structure has been remodeled as an institution for post-1945 Austrian art. A rota of temporary exhibitions take place at this steel-framed, light-infused building year round, with its basement dedicated to sculptor Fritz Wotruba's (1907–75) work. *Salon für Kunstbuch* in the foyer is a shop and also an installation by Austrian artist Bernhard Chella. Created as a 1:1 model of a bookshop, it challenges the relationships within current cultural production and offers space for public discussions and book presentations.

🕐 1100–2100 (W–Th), 1100–1800 (F–Su & P.H.)
💲 €7/5.50 🏠 Arsenalstr. 1, 1030
📞 +43 (0)1 795 571 34 📋 www.21erhaus.at

"Go there and you will see for yourself!"
– Madame Mohr

14 Wiener Art Foundation
Map A, P.102

This cultural non-profit has three exhibition venues in Vienna: two in the second district Kunstraum am Schauplatz, Büro Weltausstellung, and Galerie Kunstbüro in the sixth district, being the largest one. Directed by gallerist Amer Abbas and curator Stefan Bidner, the foundation is dedicated to opening the public's eyes to the vanguard of contemporary art and art discourse through collaborations, exhibits and self publications. Visit their website for the latest programming.

🕐 1400–1800 (M–F) or by appointment
📍 Regular location: Galerie Kunstbüro, Schadekgasse 6/9 A, 1060, +43 (0)6 991 523 1349
📞 +43 676 430 2191
🔗 www.artfoundation.at

"It has been one of the committed cultural work for years now. A low-threshold meeting point for young and established artist, and hotspot of the local art sector."
– Klemens Torggler

 TBA21
Map I, P.108

Thyssen-Bornemisza Art Contemporary's programmes never disappoint. Sitting at a lush corner of the beautiful Augarten (#8), this contemporary art centre frequently commissions ambitious projects and infuses art into every nook and canny of modern day life and the 1950s studio space, formerly of Austrian sculptor Gustinus Ambrosi. Check for happenings at David Adjaye's open-air stage and the new café Die AU. TBA21's bookshop sells stationery, bags and their own publications connected to their past projects.

🕐 1200–1700 (W–Th & P.H.), –1900 (F–Su & P.H.)
🏠 Scherzergasse 1A, 1020   📞 +43 (0)1 513 985 624
🔗 www.tba21.org

 "Afterwards one should walk through Augarten for the two huge WWII anti-aircraft gun blockhouse towers or the porcelain factory, the second oldest one in Europe."
– mischer'traxler studio

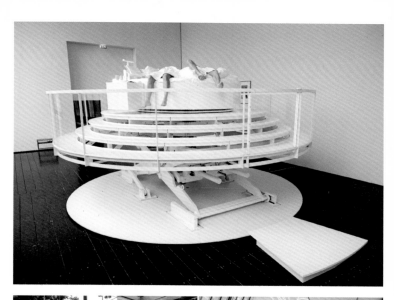

16 Kunsthistorisches Museum
Map A, P.103

An architectural twin of Museum of Natural History, just opposite, the Musuem of Art History building was originally commissioned in 1891 to shelter and showcase the Royal Habsburgs' artistic finds. Its major collection features 17th-century Flemish and early Netherlandish paintings and awaits to be explored in *Gemäldegalerie* (Picture Gallery), just above *Kunstkammer Wien* (Chamber of Art and Wonder) and the hall filled with Egyptian antiquities. Saliera, the Benvenuto Cellini sculpture in *Kunstkammer*, is known for being stolen in 2005 and recovered eight months later.

🕙 1000–1800 (F–W), –2100 (Th), closed on Monday from September to May 💲 €14/11, covers access to Neue Burg 🏠 Maria–Theresien–Pl., 1010 📞 +43 (0)1 525 240 URL www.khm.at 🖉 Special opening hours on holidays. Guided tour: €14

Peter Paul Rubens

"It has one of the most beautiful historical art collections in the world. Don't miss Gemäldegalerie."
– Klaus Mühlbauer, Mühlbauer

 17 MAK
Map O, P.110

The spacious interior of the imperial Museum of Applied Arts invites a unique collection ranging from traditional craft to overseas art. Despite the city's rich history of applied arts, this is the only museum with permanent exhibitions dedicated to the genre, alongside design and contemporary art. Highlights are pieces of the Wiener Werkstätte, its tremendous chair collection, Klimt drawings and the Margarete Schütte-Lihotzky kitchen. MAK's branch Geymüllerschlössel manifests the wealth of Biedermeier interior design and hosts MAK DESIGN SALON yearly, from May/June through to fall. Stop by MAK's design shop before you leave.

🕓 1000–2200 (Tu), 1000–1800 (W–Su)
💲 €9.90/7.50 🏠 MAK: Stubenring 5, 1010, Geymüllerschlössel: Pötzleinsdorferstr. 102, 1180
📞 +43 (0)1 711 362 48 🔗 mak.at
🎫 Guided Tours: DE: 1100 (Sa), EN: 1200 (Su), €2, Free admission: 1800–2200 (Tu) & October 26

 "Tuesday evenings (6–10pm) are MAK night with free entry. Pay a visit to Café Prückel, my favourite kaffeehaus in Vienna, which is just across the street."

– Fabienne Feltus, Bureau F

18 Rabbit Eye Movement
Map C, P.105

Started as a street art concept dedicated to all the fervent "rabbits" out on the streets, Rabbit Eye Movement is a breath of fresh air in Vienna's gallery scene. Graffitist and illustrator Nychos acknowledges the culture with this multipurpose space where the curious and the creative meet. REM is an agency, a show venue and a café in its own right. Its retail space sells unique artist-sourced merchandise, art prints and its branded clothing, featuring special editions produced to coincide artists' shows.

🕐 1200–1900 (Tu–Sa)
🏠 Gumpendorferstr. 91, 1060
☎ +43 (0)1 595 3059
🔗 rabbiteyemovement.at

"Drink some beers and have some fun."
– WILD

19 Ankerbrotfabrik
Map P, P.110

Easily accessible by tram (route 6), the former Anker Bread Factory was reborn as one of Vienna's most diverse cultural spaces. Galleries, art studios, initiatives and charity shops take over this old charming brickstone building and its courtyards to celebrate photography and performing arts. Check the facebook pages of each initiative for opening hours and events like the recurring *Mondschein Bazar*. Magdas Kantine, affiliated to Caritas, is a hip community kitchen where you can take a breather and enjoy food prepared by retired chefs and people with special needs.

🏠 *Absberggasse 27, 1010* 📞 *+43 (0)1 982 3939*
🌐 *www.brotfabrik.wien* 📘 *BROTFABRIK WIEN*

"If possible, stay until the early hours of the morning and enjoy the smell of freshly baked bread wafting through."
– DMAA

20 Arena
Map U, P.111

If you're a punk, psychobilly, ska and hardcore lover, you will find your fix at Arena. Concerts, international acts, parties, festivals, open airs and summer outdoor screenings await at this former abattoir all year round, organised by the likes of Viennese radio station FM4 and HipHop Open. Arrive at least an hour late for shows or join the rowdy crowd at one of the bars if you're early. If you're lost on the street, look for Arena's trademark chimney to guide.

🕐 🅂 *Showtimes & ticket price vary with programme*
🏠 *Baumgasse 80, 1030*
☎ *+43 (0)1 798 8595*
🔗 *DE: www.arena.co.at,*
EN: arenavienna.tumblr.com

"We played here once open air in a snowstorm, and it turned into an Austrian winter wonderland on stage!"
– GIANTREE

21 Schauspielhaus
Map L, P.109

Small but always pushing the boundaries of theatrical art, Schauspielhaus pleasantly surprises the public with original plays and experimental performances. Since 1978, it has grown from a small varieté theatre and cinema into one of the main stages in Vienna, often with colourful, eccentric stage designs to complement the acts. Expect more exciting programmes from this playhouse as young theatre directors and playwrights take up the baton and run the playhouse. The surrounding culinary options make for good hang-outs after shows!

🕐 1600-1800 (M-Sa) 💲 €19/10
🏠 Porzellangasse 19, 1090 📞 +43 (0)1 317 010 118
🔗 www.schauspielhaus.at

"It's the best innovative theatre in town. If you don't speak German, translate the description of the play from their website before you go."

– Hubert Weinheimer

22 Albertina

Map B, P.104

Standing at the heart of Vienna's art scene, Albertina holds one of the world's largest collections of old master prints, among modern graphic works, photographs and architectural drawings. Beside the special shows area, on permanent display in its palatial halls are the most exciting art movements of the last 130 years, from French impressionism to German Expressionism to the Russian avant garde. Don't leave without a visit to the terrace. Open 24/7, it offers a nice view to the Vienna State Opera and horse carriages doing their rounds.

 1000–1800 (Th–Tu), –2100 (W)
€11.9/9.7/8.5
Albertinapl. 1, 1010
+43 (0)1 534 830
www.albertina.at

"If you are here in summer (July–August), check out their ALBERT&TINA club. Also, Burggarten right next to it offers both a great restaurant and a butterfly house."

– Katie Gruber, Katie g.

23 CreativeMornings Vienna

CreativeMornings takes place in 125 different cities around the world and Vienna's falls on the last Friday of every month. Enjoy the company of local creative talent and inspiration-seekers as well as free breakfast, coffee and a short talk based on a global theme. Past topics ranged from "revolution", "ugly" to "robots", to which design legends and entrepreneurs alike have been invited to respond with reference to their expertise. Lectures are usually in English or German and venues vary with events. Announcements of upcoming events will be made on their facebook page or sent out via their mailing list which you can subscribe to online.

URL creativemornings.com/cities/vie
f CreativeMornings Vienna

"Check if there's a CreativeMornings event happening during your stay and register for a ticket the Monday before an event."

– Alice Katter, moodley brand identity

24 Stadtschrift
Map E, P.106

A brief history of Viennese retail and typographic evolution are fabricated in this vertical museum that literally welcomes visitors at any hours of the day. Initiated by Birgit Ecker and Roland Hörmann in 2014, Stadtschrift is a self-financing project set to preserve and archive antiquated shop signs as they are junked across the city. Come at the right time for a different view. Every full hour between 6pm and 9pm you can see the lit signs switch.

Kleine Sperlgasse 2c, 1020
www.stadtschrift.at Stadtschrift Vienna

"There is a sign next to the wall explaining the history of the displayed store signs."

– Andreas Scheiger

Markets & Shops

Proven glass crafts, Viennese labels and bountiful produce markets

As with most things in Vienna, when shopping you'll encounter shops where time seemingly stands still with traditional products that have rarely changed, juxtaposed with contemporary and new emerging styles and objects. Mariahilfer Straße is Vienna's largest shopping street, full of large department stores with smaller independent shops interspersed.

Visiting Altmann Kühne's confectionary (#36) in the heart of the city is an experience in itself. Located in protected cultural heritage site, their chocolates are all handcrafted, as is the packaging, designed by the legendary Wiener Werkstätte. The sweet pieces make the perfect souvenir.

Spend Saturday mornings getting lost in the city's favourite market Naschmarkt (#35), home to more than 400 different vendors. Taste white honey, dried and fresh food or falafels that Vienna's Turkish community offers. Hang out at one of the delis or walk further to find a bargain at the largest flea market in the city.

The 7th district (Neubau) is full of innovative shop concepts – pay Gebrüder Stitch (#31) a visit and have them tailor you neat organic denims, accessorise your style at meshit (#30) and finish your look with a haircut at WALL (#32) or Less is More (#27), the most atmospheric hair salon you'll find in Vienna.

For a one of a kind creation, check out Studio Alja 9er, a collective of goldsmiths known for their quirky jewellery. During your visit pop into any local supermarket to stock up on Dragee Keksi and Manner Schnitten two classic Austrian biscuits.

Polka
Product design studio

Polka stands for purpose, practicality and a certain playfulness. Started by Marie Rahm and Monica Singer, the studio tells stories through furniture, products and interior installation.

Lunzers Maß-Greißlerei

Seite Zwei
Branding & design agency

Seite Zwei comprises Stefan Mayer and Christian Begusch. Since 2011, we have created heart- and mind-driven design solutions in the fields of commercial and cultural design.

Johanna Stögmüller
Chief editor, BIORAMA

Born in upper Austria, I live and work in Vienna. BIORAMA is a magazine about sustainable lifestyle, where I tell about my world and reflect on simple and solid values.

J. & L. Lobmeyr

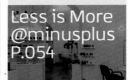

Less is More @minusplus

Ronnie Boehm
Photographer

My work focuses heavily on dance. I'm a knowledge junkie who's passionate about food, ballet, muay thai, science, music and travelling.

Buchhandlung Walther König

Wolfgang Lehrner
Artist

Through cinematic portraits of everyday urban life, Lehrner investigates and responds to the developments of cities and the seemingly insignificant similarities between them.

Patrycja Domanska
Product designer

I'm a Polish designer and I've been running my design practice here since 2010. I'm obsessed with lighting design. Some of my work are collected by the Museum of Applied Arts, Vienna.

Westbahnstraße

meshit

Mike Lanner & Moriz Piffl
Founders, Gebrüder Stitch

We are an Austrian manufacturer of made-to-measure organic jeans. Our goal is to rouse into people's consciousness the value of a product, and delight them with well-fitted clothes.

Gebrüder Stitch Concept Store
P.058

WALL
P.060

MOTSA
DJ & Producer

I love it when people do what they do passionately. If I'm not making music or DJ'ing, I'll be enjoying good food, testing ideas in the kitchen, or out for a stroll to restart my brain.

Vandasye
Design studio

Vandasye is Peter Umgeher and Georg Schnitzer. Ranging from industrial products to exhibition design, Vandasye's work centres around utility and the evolution of domestic behaviour.

Rave Up Records
P.061

Strukt GmbH
Design studio

We specialise in interaction, motion and graphics design. Since 2007, we've realised media installations and animations for exhibitions, corporate and cultural events.

Brunnenmarkt
P.062

Naschmarkt
P.064

MARCH GUT
Industrial design studio

MARCH GUT is Christoph March and Marek Gut who are committed to marrying new technology and environmental sustainability. Specialties include exhibition facility and furniture design.

Alfredo Barsuglia
Artist

Vienna has been my home base since 1998, although I had also spent some years abroad time and again. I still travel very often, and always return to Vienna with great pleasure.

Altmann & Kühne
P.065

25 J. & L. Lobmeyr
Map B, P.104

Still a family-own business, now in the hands of the sixth generation, glass manufacturer Lobmeyr has earned its international acclaim for producing the first electric chandelier with Thomas Edison in 1883 and keeping their craft in fashion since 1823. Lobmeyr glass is wonderfully thin. In the artistic aspect, many historical pieces were co-developed with painters, architects and designers like Adolf Loos, Stefan Sagmeister, Helmut Lang and Tomas Alonso. Amongst them some are collected by world museums like MoMA, Cooper Hewitt and MAK.

🕐 1000–1900 (M–F), –1800 (Sa)
🏠 Kärntner Str. 26, 1010
☎ +43 (0)1 512 050 888
URL www.lobmeyr.at
⊘ Shop closes on public holidays

"Take time to wander and dive into the sparkling wonder world."
– Polka

26 Lunzers Maß-Greißlerei

Map G, P.107

Pay a visit to Lunzers even if you have tried package-free shopping elsewhere. Beginning life as a constructive response to modern convenience, this modern grocery sells locally produced organic food and ecological cleaning products as loose pieces or in reusable containers which you can bring back for future use. Offerings are updated by season, and the range includes cheeses, bread, fruit, sausages, oil and greens. If you are not after food, you can still come for hoppers and reusable jars. Their in-house bar area serves lunch, soup and coffee every day.

🕐 0900–1900 (M–F), –1700 (Sa)
🏠 Heinestr. 35, 1020 📞 +43 (0)1 212 1387
URL www.mass-greisslerei.at
🖉 Shop may take summer break

"Bring your own vessels to fill them up or buy some at the store. They are also offering drinks and little snacks at their bar."

– Seite Zwei

27 Less is More @minusplus

Map A, P.102

When Mies' design philosophy is applied to haircare, it becomes high-quality, functional hair products that are beneficial to both the environment and your own health. Organic cosmetics are not a new idea, but Less Is More dedicate themselves to innovating shampoo, styling and special care formulas by combining certified organic ingredients, biomimetic principles, aromatherapy with the stylist-founders' expertise. The brand is against animal testing, and their products can be acquired from one of their three studios, named minusplus.

🕙 1000–1900 (Tu–W), –2000 (F), –1500 (Sa), –1800 (M & Th)
🏠 Kirchengasse 22, 1070
📞 +43 (0)1 956 9549
URL www.lessismore.at, www.minusplus.company

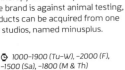

"Organic haircare at its best! Get yourself a new haircut or simply try out their products. You and your hair will love it."

– Johanna Stögmüller, BIORAMA

28 Westbahnstraße
Map A, P.102

As more camera shops, print labs and galleries crowd into Westbahnstraße, this mecca for photography enthusiasts is in the heart of Neubau. Photography students, artists, designers and publishers regularly flock to the area for professional supplies and advice, or visit the prominent WestLicht gallery, where a rota of Viennese and international photographers display their work. Take your time to also roam the secondhand shops, bike stores and little cafés that line the street.

🕑 WestLicht: 1100–1900 (F–W), –2100 (Th)
🏠 Westbahnstr. 40, 1070
🌐 www.westlicht.com
🖉 Gallery may take summer break

"If you are a photographer, go there."
– Ronnie Boehm

29 Buchhandlung Walther König
Map A, P.103

Walther König is an unmissable destination at MuseumsQuartier, where the Vienneses gather for cultural sparks. With chapters across Europe, König's Vienna outpost carries extensive book selection on design, fashion, photography and architecture that takes hours to explore it all. The bookseller is also a respected art book publisher itself. Key publications include the ongoing Hans Ulrich Obrist Conversation Series and artist monographs.

🕐 1000–1900 (M–Sa), 1200– (Su)
🏠 Museumspl. 1, 1070
📞 +43 (0)1 512 858 80
📘 Buchhandlung Walther Koenig Wien

"It's the biggest, best and friendliest art bookstore in town. Get lost and find something new."
– Wolfgang Lehrner

30 meshit
Map A, P.102

Since 2010, after graduating from Fashion Institute of Vienna, Hetzendorf, Ida Steixner and Lena Krampf have been playfully *meshing* geometric shapes, textured fabrics and styles to celebrate the diversity of body types. Lean or curvy you'll find pieces to create a dandy look here. On top of meshit's latest collections, get your hands on special collaborations, photobooks, magazines and accessories exclusively available at this spot.

🕐 1100–1900 (Th–F), –1800 (Sa)
🏠 Westbahnstr. 25, 1070
📞 +43 (0)6 508 945 563
URL meshit.at
🔖 Shop may take summer break

"*meshit is a great Vienna-based fashion label that everybody should know! You won't get their stuff everywhere, so take this occassion!*"

– Patrycja Domanska

31 Gebrüder Stitch Concept Store

Map A, P.103

Mike and Mo know how to flatter your curves with perfectly made denims. Using only organic cotton, Gebrüder Stitch guarantees all their jeans are products of Vienna – manually hemmed by a select team in their "Street Fair Factory" as well as their concept store "Arschsalon (Arse-Salon)" where measurements are taken. Feel free to bring your own favourite pairs to inspire them, or choose from your desired cut to thread colour and embroidery among many other optional details. Basic design takes about three weeks to complete and starts around EUR260.

🕐 1000-2000 (M-W),
   –2100 (Th-F), –1800 (Sa)
🏠 Mariahilfer Str. 4, 1070
☎ +43 (0)6 801 449 385
URL www.gebruederstitch.at

"Here you'll get jeans made to measure plus many more nice products made by the Gebrüder Stitch."
– Mike Lanner & Moriz Piffl, Gebrüder Stitch

 WALL
Map A, P.102

WALL's blend of indie designer clothing, homeware, books and skincare products beckons a highbrow following with an eye to great quality and design. Viennese organic skincare brand Lederhaas, fashion label Brandmair, San Francisco hatmaker Goorin Brothers, Barbara I Gongini from Copenhagen and Berlin shoemaker Trippen – all a reflection of owner and hair stylist extraordinaire Andreas Wall's low-key cool ethos that works for both women and men. If you wish to match your new look with Andreas' cut, make sure you book him two weeks ahead of your visit.

🕐 1100–1900 (M-F), –1700 (Sa)
🏠 Westbahnstr. 5A, 1070
📞 +43 (0)1 524 4728 URL www.kaufhauswall.com
✎ Shop closes on Monday from June to August

"If you're a fan of unusual and edgy clothes then this is the place to come to. Andreas is my favourite hairdresser and a master of his art."
– MOTSA

33 Rave Up Records
Map C, P.105

There's nothing like a big black shiny disc in a pungent old package to illicit memories and nostalgia. This has allowed Rave Up Records to withstand time. Insiders count on their vast and special selection and their exhaustive music knowledge to seek out their conscious or subconscious want, by the established or the unknown, and of genres from electro to jazz and punk rock. Their squared green bag with a screaming guy print is a commonly recognised symbol of one's interest in Vienna's music scene.

🕙 1000–1830 (M–F), –1700 (Sa)
🏠 Hofmühlgasse 1, 1060
☎ +43 (0)1 596 9650   ⨍ Rave Up Records
🔗 Shop may occasionally close on Mondays

"Music to touch."
– Vandasye

34 Brunnenmarkt
Map F, P.106

Eschewing tourists, the Brunnenmarkt is truly a farmers market for the locals. The sight of kebab restaurants and Börek stall along the street is indicative of the Turkish neighbourhood that help shape the market. Yppenplatz square towards the end of the Brunnengasse is a local gem where you can dine and enjoy the sun without being disturbed by the hustle and bustle of traffic. Have breakfast at An-do and start your stroll before 10 in the morning for the freshest produce. After that, look for Halis Börek behind the stalls to relish the best potato Börek in town.

🕑 0600-1830 (M-F), 0600-1400 (Sa)
🏠 Brunnengasse, 1160

"On saturday mornings a great variety of fresh produce and fruit. Come early, since some of the farmers only have limited supply."
– Strukt GmbH

35 Naschmarkt
Map A, P.103

Walk from stall to stall in this colossal market to find fresh organic fruit and vegetables, local eats and international delicacies. It's always packed as it's one of the city's popular hangouts and dining spots. The weekly flea market is held on Saturdays, where you can pay a visit to the many (some self-proclaimed) antique dealers there. Experienced or lucky shoppers alike, will always find a bargain on amazing goods. The market becomes an unofficial open gallery on Sunday after sunset. If you are not afraid to walk along the empty alleys in the dark, you will see a lot of artistic works painted on the shops' closed shutters.

🕐 0600-1930 (M-F), -1700 (Sa)
🏠 Naschmarkt, 1060
📞 +43 (0)1 240 555
URL www.naschmarkt-vienna.com

"Great place to spend time after a shopping tour at the Mariahilferstraße."

– Marek Gut & Christoph March, MARCH GUT

36 Altmann & Kühne
Map B, P.104

This 1928 institute is a work of masters inside-out. Its interior was designed by architect Josef Hofmann and still retaining its original state. The packaging, as hatboxes and chest of drawers in delicate wrapping paper, is a work of art by Wiener Werkstätte. The most essential of all is the chocolates, each hand crafted from nought, marzipan and cocoa until today. Satisfy your sweet tooth with Liliput, their miniature specialty, which also makes for a lovely gift in those euphoric boxes, or "Naschkasterl" as people call them in Viennese.

🕐 0900–1830 (M–F), –1700 (Sa)
🏠 Am Graben 30, 1010
📞 +43 (0)1 533 0927
URL www.altmann-kuehne.at

"Not only is it standing at one of the most beautiful spots in Vienna, but also an attraction in itself. Try the delicious and incredible small Liliput."

– Alfredo Barsuglia

Restaurants & Cafés

Time-honoured cafés, delectable schnitzels and international eats

Once capital of the expansive Austro-Hungarian empire, Viennese cuisine is influenced by the many ethnic groups that used to once call it the most important city in the empire. The cafés are where daily life happens and where intellectuals and creatives alike debate worldly matters such as Palmenhaus (#47) and Café Malipop (#46).

Enjoy a variety of bread that can be found in the plentiful corner bakeries as well as the crispy crust and fluffy pastry insides, un-equalled in Europe. Try a classic Vienna breakfast, which comes served with sweet Apricot jam and a soft-boiled egg to spoon out. Vienna has a sweet tooth and you'll find evidence of this in dishes served for breakfast, lunch and afternoon tea. Apricot dumplings, for example, or *Kaiserschmarrn*, a sweet shredded pancake often served with preserved plums or other fruit are amongst some of the most popular dishes.

Vienna's food scene shows how age-old establishments evolve to keep up with new trends. Conditorei Sluka (#40), founded in 1891 now offers gluten and lactose free options. The century old Café Korb (#38) now has an art lounge and futuristic bathroom, designed by Manfred Wolf-Plottegg. And whilst embracing modernity, both Café Korb and Conditorei Sluka offer the traditional and obligatory Mehlspeisen, including Sacher tarte and world famous apple strudel.

For a good savory option, drop into SAPA (#42), enjoy the cosy atmosphere and garden at Silberwirt (#41) or experience the taste pleasures at Heuer (#45). Local vegans go for Harvest (#44) or erna B (#37) and your best bet for some international flair is Chinese cuisine at Mama Liu & Sons (#43) or Hotel am Brilliantengrund (#39) for Filipino fare.

BOKEHdesignstudio
Design studio

We work mainly in the field of 3D visualisation but also create animation and graphic design. We make things look nice.

Café Korb
P.072

Benjamin Quirico
Fashion editor & designer

I write about fashion, sex, life and love in Vienna, which can be read in FAUX FOX and Volume Magazine. I'm also a cat lover and designer for my label, Szimon+Rosenthal and clients.

Clemens Fantur
Music journalist

I moved from the mountains of Tyrol to Vienna in 2000. I practise photography and contribute to Radio FM4, an Austrian radio station for alternative music.

erna B
P.070

Hotel am Brillanten-grund
P.073

Mira Kolenc
Ein Feldforschungsprojekt

Born and raised in Bavaria, I felt my love for a vintage lifestyle and decided to look like one of the women in Federico Fellini's movies at 16. My blog discusses the roles of both sexes today.

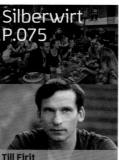

Silberwirt
P.075

Till Firit
Founder, MONO VERLAG

I'm from Germany and started living in Vienna ten years ago. Vienna's slow rhythm of life, rich cultural resources and high quality of life make her a great place to live and work.

Ákos Major
Photographer

Major is a photographer from Budapest, Hungary, shooting natural and manmade land-scapes with cameras produced by Mamiya, Silvestri and Wista.

Conditorei Sluka
P.074

SAPA
P.076

atelier olschinsky
Design studio

Peter Olschinsky and Verena Weiss are passionate about illustration, photography and graphic design. To them, working with dedicated people is essential for staying fresh and motivated.

Mama Liu & Sons
P.078

Harvest
P.079

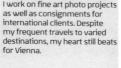

Klaus Pichler
Photographer

I work on fine art photo projects as well as consignments for international clients. Despite my frequent travels to varied destinations, my heart still beats for Vienna.

Eva Fischer
Founder, sound:frame festival

I became interested in the connection between sound and image in school. Since 2007, I organise and curate sound:frame that features audiovisual exhibitions and performances.

Heuer am Karlsplatz
P.080

Katharina Unger
Founder, Livin Studio

I am an Austrian born industrial designer and founded Livin Studio. My design of an insect breeding machine took me all around the world to discuss entomophagy (eating insects).

Café Malipop
P.081

Palmenhaus
P.082

dottings™
Industrial design studio

Since 2006, Sofia Podreka and Katrin Radanitsch have teamed up to innovate products, lighting and spaces with select specialists. Their designs are elegant and responsibly produced.

BOICUT
Artist

I moved to Vienna about 12 years ago and still am in love with the city, especially in spring and summer.

Disco Volante
P.083

37 erna B
Map D, P.105

erna B connects to owner Elisabeth Bader's roots in every way, beginning with the shop's name – a tribute to her beloved grandmother. She collected the café and bar's chairs from a fire station and the light fixtures from an ice rink in her hometown. Referencing granny's recipes, homemade vegetarian light meals and vegan cakes are a reflection of her meatless diet and love for pastries. Enjoy an apple and poppy seed cake or Austrian sandwich at the outdoor sitting set in a tranquil neighbourhood. At night, grab a lager on tap from the cozy bar.

🕐 1500–0100 (Tu–Th), 1400–0100 (F–Sa), –0000 (Su)
🏠 Große Neugasse 31, 1040
📞 +43 (0)660 392 5961 URL www.ernab.at

"Best coffee, delicious cakes, vegan food, nice people, great staff."

– BOKEHdesignstudio

38 Café Korb
Map B, P.104

Judging by photos on the wall taken decades ago, this legendary café looks nothing like when it was first opened in 1904. However it does remain in original 50s fittings since the Widl's has taken over. Susanne Widl, daughter of the family and famed Austrian performance artist now runs the café and curates an art lounge complete with a futuristic bathroom designed by Manfred Wolf-Plottegg at the basement. The café's unique vibe brings together people of diverse backgrounds. Enjoy their knockout apfelstrudel while people watching.

🕐 0800–0000 (M–Sa), 1000–2300 (Su & P.H.) 🏠 Brandstätte 9, 1010
📞 +43 (0)1 533 7215
URL www.cafekorb.at

"Come here for the best Apfelstrudel in town! You may even get to meet Korb's owner, the eccentric Grand Dame of Viennese Art Society, Miss Susanne Widl!"

– Benjamin Quirico

39 Hotel am Brillantengrund
Map A, P.102

The hotel's kitchen offers Viennese and Mediterranean menus, topped with authentic homemade Filipino cuisine made by Mama Mangalino, mother of Hotel Director Marvin Mangalino. Get excited by Pinoy food's melange of bold flavours through the Bistek – Filipino steak in lemon soy sauce, or the Sisig Bangus – sizzling milkfish in ginger, red onion and chili peppers served on an iron plate. Vegetarian and vegan variations are available for most of the dishes.

🕐 Café: 0730–2200 (M–F), 0900– (Sa–Su)
🏠 Bandgasse 4, 1070 📞 +43 (0)1 523 3662
URL www.brillantengrund.com

"Its beautiful courtyard is one of the best places to enjoy your afternoon and escape the summer heat."

– Clemens Fantur

40 Conditorei Sluka
Map N, P.110

Since the 1890s, this pâtisserie and confection-ery shop's creations were sought after by both Austrian nobility and bourgeoisie who had a sweet tooth. Playwright Thomas Bernhard is among Sluka's famous guests, and he even included it in his polemical play "Heldenplatz" (1988). Located just next to the City Hall but away from tourist trails, this historic venue's intimate setting still oozes noble elegance. Try one of their specialties – Slukatorte or Sacher-torte. Their pastries also come partially gluten or lactose free.

🕐 0800-1900 (M-F), -1730 (Sa)
🏠 Rathauspl. 8, A-1010
📞 +43 (0)1 405 7172, +43 (0)1 406 8896
URL www.sluka.at

"An apricot strudel or Fruchtschüsserl or Punschkrapfen with a cup of 'großer Brauner' are all that you need for a perfect afternoon in Vienna."

– Mira Kolenc, Ein feldforschungsprojekt

41 Silberwirt
Map D, P.105

Warm summer evenings pass by quickly when you dine al fresco in Silberwirt's lush courtyard, with a cold beer in your hand and a schnitzel on your plate. It's a typical "Wiener Beisl", a Viennese neighbourhood eatery set in a historic tavern. They serve a two-course lunch menu that changes daily from Monday to Saturday at €6.2. Scrumptious picks include John Dory fillet and stuffed pork breast. A full house is common, especially on weekends, so advance reservations are recommended.

🕐 1200-0000 daily 🏠 Schloßgasse 21, 1050
📞 +43 (0)1 544 4907 🔲 www.silberwirt.at

"Come here for a decent 'Beisl'. Good Viennese dishes, good service, the beautiful garden and reasonable prices."

– Till Firit, MONO VERLAG

42 **SAPA**
Map A, P.102

SAPA is a young and chic Vietnamese restaurant, keen to add innovative twists to fresh ingredients. Expect a convivial vibe with upbeat music towards the weekend. The food is vegetarian friendly, and their dish of the day never disappoints. Try their fingerfood options, such as the Enten-Rolle – rice paper rolls with crispy duck and herbs. Main dishes like ChilliTofu and vegetarian sweet and sour soup invigorate all tastebuds. Just make sure to make reservation at least 24 hours beforehand.

🕐 1100–0000 (M-Th), –0200 (F-Sa)
🏠 Lindengasse 35, 1070
📞 +43 (0)1 526 5626
URL www.sapa.at

"Reserve a table!"
– Ákos Major

43 Mama Liu & Sons
Map A, P.103

Traditional oriental décor is nowhere to be found in this hipster-Chinese restaurant. In a modish industrial setting, the only hint to the cuisine served here is the raw brick wall's mural of the ancients. Available with both meat and vegetarian soup base, hotpot, or the "Chinese fondue" is their signature. Order it as a combo with a variety of dumplings, including the ones in Mama Liu's flavorsome peanut sauce. The restaurant is also equipped with a nice bar.

🕐 1200–0000 (Tu–Th, Su), – 0200 (F–Sa)
🏠 Gumpendorferstr. 29, 1060
☎ +43 (0)1 586 3673
🔗 www.mamaliuandsons.at

"Great food, cool place."
– atelier olschinsky

44 Harvest
Map E, P.106

With its friendly vibe and courteous hospitality, this cosy café and bistro only cooks vegan dishes, while still providing an organic cow's milk alternative for their house blend Fair Trade coffees. Lunch is served as a buffet, adhering to a "Slow Food, Fast Served" principle that offers lentils dhal, vegetable curry, seitan kebab sandwich and more. Don't forget to try the salads with special herbal oil dressings. For guests only after a drink, they also have a special selection of organic herb teas, homemade lemonade and regional wines.

🕐 1100-2300 (M-F), 1000-1800 (Sa-Su, P.H.)
🏠 Karmeliterpl. 1, 1020
📞 +43 676 492 7790 URL harvest-bistrot.at

> "This is the number one vegetarian restaurant in town! Check out Harvest's Sunday brunch available from 10am to 4pm."
> – Klaus Pichler

45 Heuer am Karlsplatz
Map B, P.104

Located a block away from Karlspaltz's U-Bahn, Heuer serves everything from breakfast to dinner, and smoothies to cocktails. The restaurant is a realisation of chef Peter Fallenbügl's culinary vision, equipped with a clay oven that makes great steckerlfisch and Maishenderlfilet. Pickled vegetables preserved on the spot are not only used in cooking but used to make refreshing Martini Shrubs at the centring bar area. Behind the glass façades is a show garden and laboratory for urban farming, operated by Karls Garten to raise awareness of sustainable lifestyle. Heuer carries a broad creative programme of events, check out their website to see what's on.

🕙 1000–0200 daily
🏠 Treitlstr. 2, 1040   📞 +43 (0)1 890 0590
URL www.heuer-amkarlsplatz.com

"Heuer has everything you need – amazing organic food and drinks, great music and a very nice staff!"
– Eva Fischer, sound:frame festival

46 Café Malipop
Map H, P.107

If you are looking for a truly laid back, smoky pub with great music and simple snacks, Café Malipop is the place. Owner Margit Wolf, who has been running the café for more than a quarter of a century now, is also the chef, bartender and DJ – and she does not take casual song requests. The strictly vinyl playlist includes anything from the classics of 60s and 70s to the more recent rock and indie. Dim lighting and cozy sofas are all you need to relax and enjoy a drink. Just be sure not to get too loud to disrupt the music according to informal house rules.

🕐 1930–0200 (M–Tu), –0400 (W–Sa)
📍 Ungargasse 10, 1030   📞 +43 (0)1 713 3441

> *"The owner only play vinyls and each one until the end of the record! Make sure you treat her leather sofas nicely otherwise she can get a bit angry."*
> – Katharina Unger, Livin Studio

47 Palmenhaus
Map A, P.103

Palmenhaus provides a small oasis while offering a great view overlooking another one – the quaint Burggarten – through its imposing steel and glass structure. Enjoy delightful "Wiener Frühstück" breakfast in a sun-filled setting, while the lunch and dinner menus are a mix of classical Austrian as well as Italian fine dining with a fresh selection of seafood. Do order a chocolate cake and panna cotta to wrap up the meal. The Butterfly House is just next door, and the National Library and the Vienna State Opera are one block away from both ends of the glass house.

🕐 1000–0000 (M–Th), –0100 (F–Sa), –2300 (Su & P.H.) 🏠 Burggarten 1, 1010
📞 +43 (0)1 533 1033 URL www.palmenhaus.at

"Admire the wonderful steel and glass construction, then proceed to the Imperial Butterfly House in the same building."

– Katrin Radanitsch & Sofia Podreka, dottings™

48 Disco Volante
Map C, P.105

Plain wooden chairs, small tables in rows and bare white walls captures the clean and crisp interior of a southern Italian pizzeria. Yet you can hardly say the spot is unadorned – every guest's attention is drawn to the wood fired pizza oven which apart from offering a genuine taste of Naples, is also a giant sparkling disco ball. A single-page menu concludes what it is like to dine in an Italian pizzeria – simple and basic, but with top ingredients either with or without tomato sauce. Try the Bufala with perfectly ripe tomatoes and the original buffalo mozzarella, or the Egidio for meat lovers.

🕐 1200–0000 (M–Sa), –2300 (Su & P.H)
🏠 Gumpendorferstr. 98, 1060
📞 +43 664 195 2545 URL www.disco-volante.at
🖉 Pizza supply suspends during 1500–1800 (Tu–F) and one hour before closing

"This is one of the best pizza places in Vienna with local/ original Italian ingredients. Make a reservation beforehand if you're going in a group of more than two."

– BOICUT

Nightlife
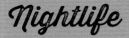

Local brews, groovy DJs and progressive line-ups

Vienna's burgeoning cultural happenings do not cease after dark. Amidst vivacious partying, its bars, clubs and lounges are often venues of exhibitions, poetry slams and stalwarts of cutting-edge live performances. The city's nightlife embraces the Viennese mentality – laid back and easygoing. Most clubs do not require a particular dress code, but beware sneakers are still frowned upon at fancier locations.

Commence your evening with an unconventional heriger dinner and Austrian jukebox music at the quirky Zum Gschupftn Ferdl (#54) and sip cocktails after at the modern If Dogs Run Free (#53). Dance the night away at Pratersauna's (#49) poolside or Tanzcafé Jenseits' (#55) intimate dance floor. If you're in the mood for a DJ night, check out brut im Künstlerhaus (#59). Come 4am if you're still standing, or get a Käsekrainer at Donau (#50) to ease your hunger.

There are areas in the city with multiple options for a fun night. For a mix of cultural vibes and party spirit, head to Karlsplatz, the town square, or the Gürtel, a ring road dotted with bars, clubs and live music venues. Among them is the rhiz (#51) featuring Viennese electronic music, and CHELSEA, an eclectic venue that hosts DJs and shows football matches on big screens. Towards the end of summer, the Gürtel Nightwalk (www.guertelnightwalk.at) brings shows onto the road for a buzzing crowd. Start with a concert at Musikverein.

HVOB
Band

Established in 2012, HVOB (Her Voice Over Boys) is Viennese producers and electronic music duo, Anna Müller and Paul Wallner.

Pratersauna
P.088

Donau
P.090

breadedEscalope
Industrial design collective

BreadedEscalope is Sascha Mikel, Martin Schnabl and Michael Tatschl, whose approaches address socio economic issues and cultural relevance about artefacts and space.

SEX JAMS
Band

Hi, there! We're a noise-pop band from Vienna. We like records, nature, Asian food, cemeteries and writing music. At night we watch shows or hang out with beer cans in hand.

rhiz
P.091

LWZ Design & Animation
Design & animation studio

LWZ experiments with unconventional approaches that bring visuals derailments happy endings.

The Loft
P.092

If Dogs Run Free
P.094

Tzoulubroth
Architectural duo

Originally from New York and Taiwan, Chieh-shu Tzou and Gregorio Lubroth have made Vienna their home. In a city not lacking in inspiration, they aim to inspire by breaking the rules.

Renate Stoica
Founder, Dadarena

My label literally stands for "unique worlds of wearable images". At my workshop on the city's edge, I make silkscreen prints onto fabrics and turn artworks into clothes.

Zum
Gschupftn
Ferdl
P.095

Lilli Hollein
Co-founder, Vienna Design Week

Lilli Hollein was born in Vienna and has always loved the place. She studied industrial design, works as a curator and has published widely and internationally on architecture and design.

Garten-baukino P.097

Stadtschrift
Curators

We are Birgit Ecker and Roland Hörmann. Beginning as an initiative to preserve Vienna's typographic heritage, we rescue, document and exhibit the city's historic façade signs.

studio VIE
Branding & design agency

studio VIE is a branding and design agency founded by Eva Oberdorfer, Anouk Rehorek and Christian Schlager. Life is about "VIE", and VIE works by instinct.

Tanzcafé Jenseits P.096

Transporter P.098

SOYBOT
Micro publishing collective

SOYBOT members share an affinity to graphics, illustration and hardware. Their work and prints are published in small editions, on the most elementary topics like tribals and UFOs.

brut im Künstler-haus P.100

Pilot Jr.
Band

We are a dream-pop band, consisting of five young musicians based in Vienna. Each of us comes from a different background, but are united through the music and the city.

The Boys You Know
Band

We're a four-piece alternative rock band, weaned on indie rock giants like Dinosaur Jr., the Lemonheads and Pavement. We're all between 20 and 25 and have released two albums thus far.

Eternal Laser P.099

Nightfly's P.101

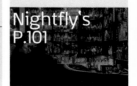

49 Pratersauna
Map J, P.108

Being a former sauna awarded Pratersauna a garden pool that is beautifully lit at night and opened for afternoon dive-ins during summer. Another summer happening is the legend-ary Prater Unser, where top electro-, techno-, house-performers around the world play for a weekend in July. The refurbished 60s premises is a no-fuss party and art space for a relaxed, hip crowd. The variety of nights here spans being mesmerised at a visual gig, dancing in frenzy at a themed club night and attending a multimedia art exhibition.

🕐 2300–0600 (Th–Sa, Oct–Apr), 2100– (W–Su, May–Sep), Pool: 1300–2100 (W–Sa, Jun, Sep)
🏠 Waldsteingartenstr. 135, 1020
📞 +43 (0)1 729 1927 🔗 www.pratersauna.tv

"The Prater Unser festival that Pratersauna hosts yearly in early July makes the best weekend in Vienna."
– HVOB

50 **Donau**
Map A, P.103

Donau is a techno bar complete with an in-house Würstelstand and cable cars repurposed as smoking rooms. The pleasantly bizarre Alice in Wonderland setting is dreamier when the plain high ceiling and arched beams are creatively lit by mesmerising projection. The spacious bar area serves strong drinks at reasonable prices. What more can you ask for than a Käsekrainer at 4am after you've had a couple of Long Islands down. It may take some time to locate the unmarked bar entrance. Follow the techno beats for hints.

🕑 2000-0400 (M-Th), -0600 (F-Sa), -0200 (Su)
🏠 Karl Schweighofer Gasse 10, 1070
URL www.donautechno.com

"The circular bar makes it easy to make new eye contacts. Try to find the entrance."
– breadedEscalope

51 rhiz

Map F, P.106

Located beside the car-filled Neulerchenfelder
Straße and right under the U-Bahn rail, music
at the rhiz always interacts with buzzing
traffic. This glorious venue set the stage for
Vienna's experimental electronic scene and
continues to thrive. The daily DJ programme
starts at about 9pm, and regular live gigs never
fail to stun the rather intimate space. Every August, rhiz is one of the major participant of the
Gürtel Nightwalk, where cars willingly make
way for some 20 stages set on the long city
ring road for local and international alternative
music, including one right outside the bar.

🕐 1800 till late daily   🏠 U–Bahnbogen 37, 1080
📞 +43 (0)1 409 2505   URL rhiz.org

*"Lots of good bands play there. Not a big venue
but a nice bar."*

– SEX JAMS

52 **The Loft**
Map F, P.106

The Loft says they are making better parties in Vienna. If the first goal is diversity then they have succeeded. Situated directly on Gürtel, The Loft occupies three floors. A friendly ground floor café holds movie nights, mini acoustic concerts and monthly poetry slams for the cultural crowd. Go either up or down one floor you can choose to sit comfortably at a lounge area, or dance to bumping music ranges from hip hop, funk, rock to the unclassified. Check online for themed parties and DJ line-ups.

🕑 1900–0200 (Tu–Th), 2000–0400 (F–Sa)
🏠 Lerchenfeldergürtel 37, 1160
📞 +43 (0)1 947 7619 🌐 www.theloft.at

"Ask for a 'Zirbenschnaps' there. The owner always has a handmade bottle of it near the bar."

– LWZ Design & Animation

53 If Dogs Run Free
Map A, P.103

"If dogs run free, then why not we." – guests' imagination would probably run free when they try to interpret the cocktail bar's imposing faceted ceiling. Designed by Vienna-based Tzou Lubroth Architekten, also partners of the bar, the ceiling is intended to be an off-the-wall gallery space and the spiky installation, the first of an art series to come. The bar sticks to a small menu of classic mix, but has also succeeded in trying new things. Corpse Reviver, Russian Cocaine are examples of the weekly specials that live up to their names. The bar uses quality liquor which factors into the price of drinks.

◷ 1800–0200 (M–Th), –0400 (F–Sa)
⌂ Gumpendorfer Str. 10, 1060
☎ +43 (0)1 913 2132
URL www.ifdogsrunfree.com

"Ask the bartenders for the weekly specials and talk to your neighbour at the bar since this a perfect place to meet new people from all walks of life."

– Chieh-shu Tzou & Gregorio Lubroth, Tzoulubroth

54 Zum Gschupftn Ferdl
Map A, P.103

Zum Gschupftn Ferdl is a fun and modern interpretation of the Austrian heuriger culture. While the wine bar's pixel art décor runs counter to the image of a tavern, their simple wooden benches stay true to their heritage. The wine and liquor are organic and local, as are the cold-cuts, cheeses and spreads on their signature platters. The bar's jukebox is a treasure trove of Austrian music, where one can flip through 30s Hans Moser songs to electronic music from Affine Records. Also check online for live shows from Thursday to Saturday nights.

🕐 1600–0200 (M–Sa)
🏠 Windmühlgasse 20, 1060
📞 +43 (0)1 966 3066
📘 ZumGschupftnFerdl

"If you like the typical heuriger, you may love their unconventional fresh Viennese water. Order a mug, it looks pretty and goes well with the heuriger wine."

– Renate Stoica, Dadarena

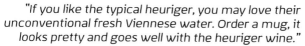

55 **Tanzcafé Jenseits**
Map A, P.102

Be prepared to indulge in a world juxtaposed with red velvet, swing dances and trashy music when you set foot in Tanzcafé Jenseits, which literally translate as "Dance Café Beyond". Intoxicating soft lighting and a setting makes guests feel so at ease that they don't hold back when getting their feet moving on the intimate dance floor. This brothel turned bar serves one of the most diverse crowds in Vienna's night scene. Just take a seat at the bar and order a martini or whiskey. You might make interesting acquaintances.

🕐 2000–0400 (Tu–Sa)
🏠 Nelkengasse 3, 1060   📞 +43 (0)1 587 1233
URL www.tanzcafe-jenseits.com

"The name Tanzcafé Jenseits makes perfect sense, because Viennese love flirting with the concept of death and afterlife. I've been visiting for 20 years."

– Lilli Hollein, Vienna Design Week

56 Gartenbaukino

Map B, P.104

With its enormous screen, some 700 seats on a non-sloped floor and original interior since its grand opening in 1960, Gartenbaukino is one of Vienna's remaining Einsaalkino. This grand theatre hall takes you back to the days when movie-going was something special – even if one has to watch between heads at times. Named after its former resident, k.u.k. Horticulture Society, the city's epicentre of film runs a programme of independent productions, timeless classics and (occasionally) mainstream blockbusters. Besides a venue for major film festivals like the Viennale, it also regularly holds smaller-scale, but equally interesting themed screenings like the Schinken series.

🕐 1600–2300 (M–Su)
📍 Parkring 12, 1010 📞 +43 (0)1 512 2354
🌐 www.gartenbaukino.at

"Its original interior is incomparable! All films shown are original versions."

– Birgit Ecker and Roland Hörmann, Stadtschrift

57 Transporter
Map D, P.105

Located not far from designer shops and galleries on the Schleifmühlgasse, Transporter is a quaint hangout for a predominantly creative crowd. Its interior is somewhat seedy but not lacking an artistic vibe. Enjoy a nice selection of beer, organic drinks and good chat with friends in the relatively relaxed non-event evenings. Music lovers usually flood in towards the weekend for live gigs, which feature a variety of indie bands and local DJs. Ping-pong is always held on a Wednesday night.

🕐 1900–0200 (Tu–Sa)
🏠 Kettenbrückengasse 1, 1050
URL www.transporterbar.at
f Transporter

"You should come here on a Wednesday for a game of table tennis with 20 other tipsy people."
– studio VIE

58 Eternal Laser

Experience Vienna's underground music scene by going to one of Eternal Laser's concerts. The music label set the stage for weirdo and synthpunk bands, and combinations of crankiness and sophistication that simply cannot be fitted into any particular genre. Both local and international line-ups perform in mutable concert venues including the famed Venster 99 and rhiz. Check out Eternal Laser's Facebook page for regular event updates as well as their online shop for the limited edition cassette tapes and prints they produce.

URL eternallaser.tumblr.com/ ananas.tictail.com
f eternallaser

"They organise music concert series and label focusing on weirdo and synthpunk."
— SOYBOT

59 brut im Künstlerhaus
Map B, P.104

Other than an open-minded programme of concerts, theatre and dance performances, the 160-seat hall space is equipped with a "brut deluxe bar" for in-between hangouts, DJ nights, as well as tailored events that sometimes extend the celebration to the whole premises. Don't expect the crowds to show up earlier than midnight, but once the party kicks off, its dance floor will be hyped up until the next morning. The space serves as a meeting hub on the Karlsplatz where cultural institutions like Musikverein and Vienna Secession are just around the corner. The other brut in Konzerthaus is a smaller theatre space reserved for specific production formats.

🕐 *Bar: Opens one hour before evening events*
🏠 *Karlspl. 5, 1010* 📞 *+43 (0)1 587 8774*
 www.brut-wien.at

"It has a great performance theatre, great concerts and great parties! If everything's closed, there might be a chance that the brut is still open."
– Pilot Jr.

60 Nightfly's
Map B, P.104

Get soaked up in the classy vibe of 50s old America in Nightfly's. The atmospheric bar and cigar lounge has a ceiling tall shelf full of spirits and liquors, as well as knowledgeable bartenders that create an extensive selection of delectable cocktails that the bar is known for. After a night of booze in soft lighting, with American Jazz and Soul music playing in the background, one would start to believe that members of the Rat Pack would grace into the bar any minute for a Jack on the Rocks.

🕐 2000–0200 (Su-Th), –0400 (F–Sa), Summer time: Su-Tu closed
🏠 Dorotheergasse 14, 1010
📞 +43 699 171 287 67 🌐 nightflys.at

"Escape the Vienna coffee house culture at this American-style bar with very little light, great drinks and Sinatra in the background."

– The Boys You Know

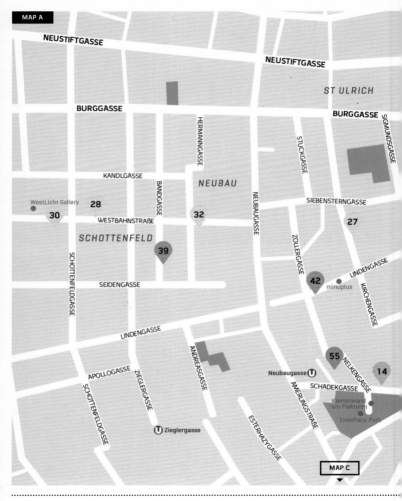

MAP A

MAP C

- 14_Wien Art Foundation (Galerie Kunstbüro)
- 27_Less is More @minusplus
- 28_Westbahnstraße
- 30_meshit
- 32_WALL
- 39_Hotel am Brillantengrund
- 42_SAPA
- 55_Tanzcafé Jenseits

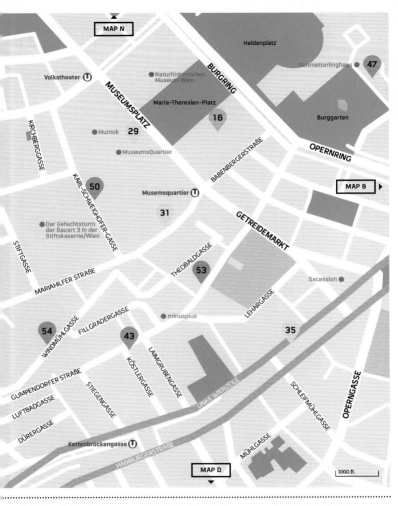

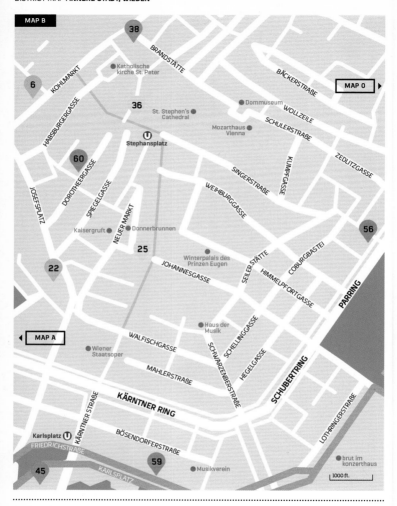

MAP B

MAP 0 ▶

◀ MAP A

- Katholische kirche St. Peter
- Dommuseum
- St. Stephen's Cathedral
- Mozarthaus Vienna
- **Stephansplatz**
- Kaisergruft
- Donnerbrunnen
- Winterpalais des Prinzen Eugen
- Haus der Musik
- Wiener Staatsoper
- **Karlsplatz**
- Musikverein
- brut im konzerthaus

1000 ft.

Streets: BRANDSTÄTTE, BÄCKERSTRAßE, KOHLMARKT, WOLLZEILE, SCHULERSTRAßE, HABSBURGERGASSE, ZEDLITZGASSE, SINGERSTRAßE, KLIMPFGASSE, JOSEFSPLATZ, DOROTHEERGASSE, SPIEGELGASSE, WEIHBURGGASSE, NEUER MARKT, SEILERSTÄTTE, COBURGBASTEI, HIMMELPFORTGASSE, PARRING, JOHANNESGASSE, SCHELLINGGASSE, WALFISCHGASSE, SCHWARZENBERGSTRAßE, HEGELGASSE, SCHUBERTRING, MAHLERSTRAße, KÄRNTNER RING, KÄRNTNER STRAße, LOTHRINGERSTRAße, BÖSENDORFERSTRAße, FRIEDRICHSTRAße, KARLSPLATZ

- 6_Retti
- 22_Albertina
- 25_J. & L. Lobmeyr

- 36_Altmann & Kühne
- 38_Café Korb
- 45_Heuer am Karlsplatz

- 56_Gartenbaukino
- 59_brut im Künstlerhaus
- 60_Nightfly's

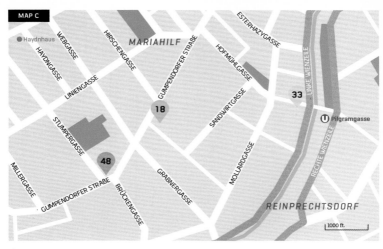

- 18_Rabbit Eye Movement
- 33_Rave Up Records
- 37_erna B
- 41_Silberwirt
- 48_Disco Volante
- 57_Transporter

DISTRICT MAPS : **LEOPOLDSTADT, OTTAKRING, JOSEFSTADT**

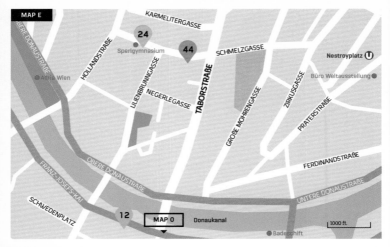

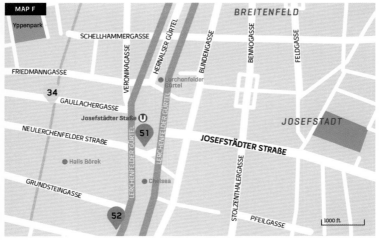

- 12_Donaukanal
- 24_Stadtschrift
- 34_Brunnenmarkt
- 44_Harvest
- 51_rhiz
- 52_The Loft

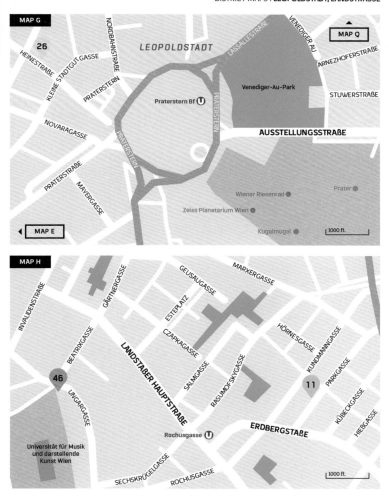

- 11_Haus Wittgenstein
- 26_Lunzers Maß–Greißlerei
- 46_Café Malipop

DISTRICT MAPS : **LEOPOLDSTADT**

- 2_Wirtschaftsuniversität Wien
- 5_Trabrennbahn Krieau
- 8_Augarten
- 15_TBA21
- 49_Pratersauna

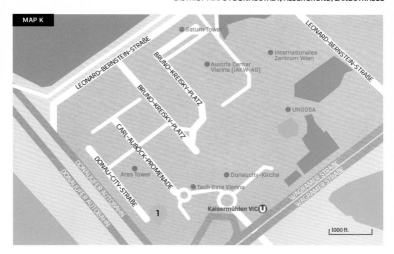

- 1_DC Towers
- 13_21er Haus
- 21_Schauspielhaus

DISTRICT MAPS : **INNERE STADT, JOSEFSTADT, FAVORITEN, LEOPOLDSTADT**

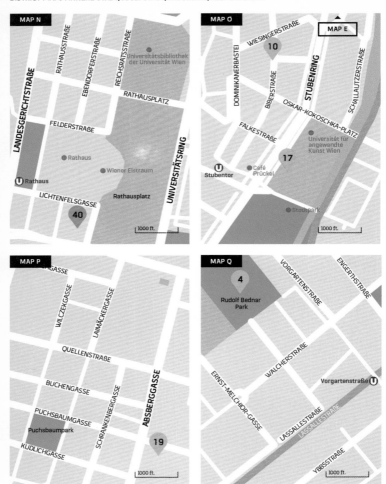

- 4_Rudolf-Bednar-Park
- 10_Österr. Postsparkasse
- 17_MAK (Museum für angewandte Kunst)
- 19_Ankerbrotfabrik
- 40_Conditorei Sluka

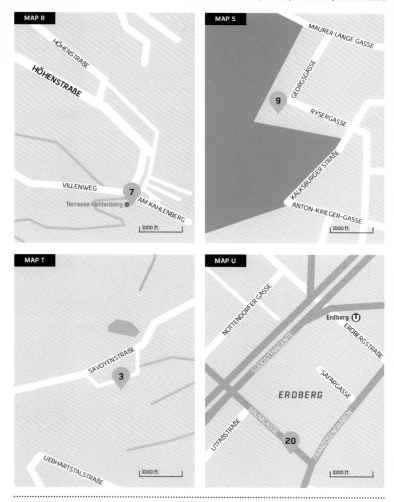

- 3_Schloss Wilhelminenberg
- 7_Kahlenberg
- 9_Wotrubakirche
- 20_Arena

Accommodations

Hip hostels, fully-equipped apartments & swanky hotels

No journey is perfect without a good night's sleep to recharge. Whether you're backpacking or on a business trip, our picks combine top quality and convenience, whatever your budget.

💲 ≤ €100 💲 €101–200 💲 €201+

The Guesthouse Vienna

The Opera, parks and grand museums are all within easy reach if you stay at this former 1960s student hostel. Traits of Viennese modern era run through the building and its 39 homey rooms and duplex suites, as Sir Terence Conran outfitted them with design classics and bespoke fittings. Enjoy the hood in its entirety with a picnic hamper prepared by their Brasserie.

🏠 Führichgasse 10, 1010   📞 +43 (0)1 512 1320
🌐 www.theguesthouse.at   💲

25hours Hotel at MuseumsQuartier

Olaf Hajek's illustrations visually brings the fantastic world of the music district into the hotel's 217 rooms. Thirty-four of which are suites with a kitchenette, and some boast a private terrace, an open-air bath and a breathtaking view on the top floor. All guests have access to MINI cars and bicycles free of charge.

 Lerchenfelder Str. 1–3, 1070   📞 *+43 (0)1 521 510*
 www.25hours-hotels.com

Urbanauts

Thanks to architects Thesi, Jonathan and Chris, vacant retail spaces at Vienna's centre now proffer an offbeat roof for nomads. The stories of now defunct blacksmith's shop, dressmaker artist studio are retained in its street lofts. Located across from the Wieden district, enjoy discounts at nearby clubs and cafés. Each room holds up to three. Price covers two bikes.

🏠 *Favoritenstr. 17/G3–5, 1040*
☎ *+43 (0)1 208 3904* 🔗 *www.urbanauts.at*

Altstadt Vienna

🏠 *Kirchengasse 41, 1070*
📞 *+43 (01) 522 6666*
🔗 *www.altstadt.at*

Meninger Downtown Franz

🏠 *Rembrandtstr. 21, 1020*
📞 *+43 (0)7 208 820 65*
🔗 *www.meininger-hotels.com/en/hotels/vienna/*

This is not a hotel

🏠 *Obere Donaustr. 9, 1020*
📞 *+43 (0)1 348 300*
🔗 *www.thisisnotahotel.at*

Hotel am Brillantengrund

🏠 *Bandgasse 4, 1070*
📞 *+43 (0)1 523 3662*
🔗 *www.brillantengrund.com*

Notes

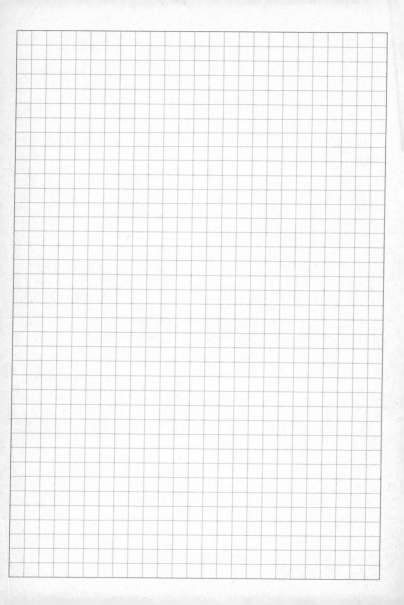

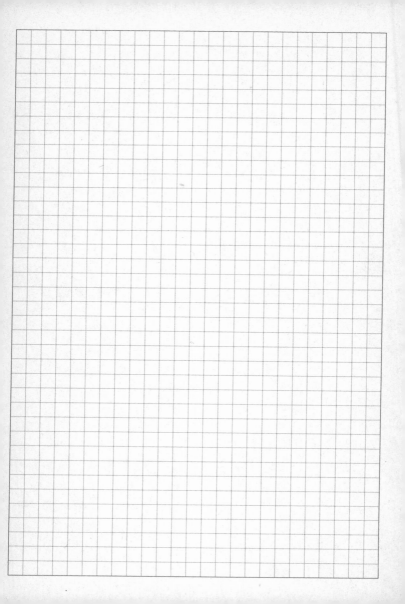

Index

Polka, *p052*
www.polkaproducts.com

Vandasye, *p061*
www.vandasye.com

Multimedia

Strukt GmbH, *p062*
www.strukt.com

Music

GIANTREE, *p042*
www.giantree.net

Hubert Weinheimer, *p044*
www.dastrojanischepferd.org
Portrait by Lemonia Lange

HVOB, *p088*
www.hvob-music.com

MOTSA, *p060*
www.motsamusic.com
Portrait: ©Jack Davison

Pilot Jr., *p100*
www.pilotjr.com

SEX JAMS, *p091*
www.motsamusic.com

Snoww Crystal, *p023*
FB: Snoww Crystal

The Boys You Know, *p101*
www.theboysyouknow.com
Portrait by JULIAN HAAS

Photography

Clemens Fantur, *p073*
itwasalladream.tumblr.com

Daniel Gebhart de Koekkoek, *p025*
www.gebhart.dk

Klaus Pichler, *p079*
www.kpic.at

Ronnie Boehm, *p055*
www.ronnieboehm.com

Ákos Major, *p076*
akosmajor.com

Publishing

Benjamin Quirico, *p072*
www.szimonrosenthal.com

Johanna Stögmüller @BIORAMA, *p054*
www.biorama.eu
Twitter: @ jstgmllr
Portrait: ©Clemens Kritzer

Mira Kolenc @Ein feldforschungsprojekt, *p074*
www.mirakolenc.com
Portrait: ©OskarSchmidt

Till Firit @MONO VERLAG, *p075*
www.monoverlag.at

Photo & other credits

brut im Künstlerhaus, *p087, 100*
(All) Florian Rainer

Eternal Laser, *p087, 099*
(All) Eternal Laser

Gartenbaukino, *p097*
(All) Astrid Ofner

Hotel am Brillantengrund, *p073, 116*
(Food & interiors) Hotel am Brillantengrund

MAK, *p038–039*
(Exterior) Gerald Zugmann/MAK
(Shop) Katrin Wißkirchen/MAK

Mama Liu & Sons, *p069, 078*
(All) atelier olschinsky

Schloss Wilhelminenberg, *p018*
(Exterior) Schloss Wilhelminenberg / austria trend

Silberwirt, *p075*
(All) Silberwirt

Pratersauna, *p084, 086, 088–089*
(Pool, parties & interior) Pratersauna

Tanzcafé Jenseits, *p087, 096*
(All) Michael Kukacka

TBA21, *p034–035*
(p034) Jakob Polacsek / TBA21, 2012
(p035 Top exhibition) Carsten Höller: LEBEN, TBA21-Augarten, 2014 (Bottom left installation) Katarina Balgavy (Open-air stage) Tereza Grandicova (Bottom right exhibition) Katarina Balgavy / TBA21, 2013

The Loft, *p092–093*
(p087 & 093 bottom left girl) Thomas Unterberger
(p092 All & p093 top, bottom music control) The Loft

In Accommodation: all courtesy of respective hotels. 25hours Hotel at MuseumsQuartier, p113 (Interior) Stephan Lemke, (MINI) courtesy of 25hours Hotel at Museums-Quartier

CITIX60

CITIx60: Vienna

First published and distributed by
viction workshop ltd

viction:ary™

7C Seabright Plaza, 9-23 Shell Street,
North Point, Hong Kong

Url: www.victionary.com
Email: we@victionary.com
▪ www.facebook.com/victionworkshop
🐦 www.twitter.com/victionary_
🐾 www.weibo.com/victionary

Edited and produced by viction:ary

Concept & art direction: Victor Cheung
Research & editorial: Queenie Ho, Caroline Kong, Eunyi Choi
Project coordination: Jovan Lip, Katherine Wong
Design & map illustration: Frank Lo

Co-curator, project coordinator & contributing writer: Katharina Unger
Contributing editor: Katee Hui
Cover map illustration: Victoria Borges
Count to 10 illustrations: Guillaume Kashima aka Funny Fun
Photography: Kollektiv Fischka (Marcell Nimfuehr, Kramer, Christine Wurnig)
Image processing: Sabine Wolf

2015 ©viction workshop ltd

Content is compiled based on facts available as of August 2015. Travellers are
advised to check for updates from respective locations before your visit.

First edition
978-988-13203-5-3
Printed and bound in China

Acknowledgements

A special thank you to all creatives, photographer(s), editor, producers, com-
panies and organisations for your crucial contributions to our inspiration and
knowledge necessary for the creation of this book. And, to the many whose
names are not credited but have participated in the completion of the book,
we thank you for your input and continuous support all along.

CITIX60
City Guides

CITIx60 is a handpicked list of hot spots that illustrates the spirit of the world's most exhilarating design hubs. From what you see to where you stay, this city guide series leads you to experience the best — the places that only passionate insiders know and go.

Each volume is a unique collaboration with local creatives from selected cities. Known for their accomplishments in fields as varied as advertising, architecture and graphics, fashion, industry and food, music and publishing, these locals are at the cutting edge of what's on and when. Whether it's a one-day stopover or a longer trip, **CITIx60** is your inspirational guide.

Stay tuned for new editions.

City guides available now:

Amsterdam
Barcelona
Berlin
Hong Kong
London
Los Angeles
Melbourne
New York
Paris
Stockholm
Tokyo
Vienna